BREAKING THE BLUES

A COMPREHENSIVE GUIDE TO MANAGING ANTIDEPRESSANT MEDICATIONS.

DR. PAUL D. RYAN

Prologue: Euphoria 7

CHAPTER 1 9

Understanding Depression 9

Causes of Depression 11

Symptoms of Depression 14

CHAPTER 2 17

Overview of Anti-Depressants 17

Mechanism of Action of Antidepressants 17

Classifications Of Anti-Depressants 18

Types Of Anti-Depressants 19

Commonly prescribed Antidepressants 21

CHAPTER 3 23

Side Effects of Anti-depressants 23

Common Side Effects 25

Rare Side Effects 26

Long-Term Side Effects 27

Benefits of Antidepressants 29

Chapter 4 33

Alternatives to Antidepressant Medications 33

Herbal Remedies 33

Cognitive Behavioral Therapy 39

Exercise 41

Daily Exercise Planner 43

Diet and Nutrition 44

Daily Diet and Nutrition Planner 46

Day 1 46

Day 2: 48

Day 3: 50

Day 4: 51

Day 6: 55

Day 7: 56

Vitamins 58

Chapter 5 61

How to Choose an Antidepressant 61

Factors to Consider When Choosing an Antidepressant 61

Real Life Example 64

Pros and Cons of Different Antidepressant .. 66

Pros of SSRIs (Selective Serotonin Reuptake Inhibitors): 66

Cons of SSRIs: 67

Pros of SNRIs (Serotonin-Norepinephrine Reuptake Inhibitors): 68

Disadvantages of SNRIs 68

Pros of Tricyclic Antidepressants: 69

Cons of Tricyclic Antidepressants: 69

Pros of MAOIs (Monoamine Oxidase Inhibitors): 70

Cons of MAOIs: 70

Questions to Ask Your Doctor 71

Chapter 6 75

How To Manage Antidepressant Syndromes 75

Identifying and Minimizing Side Effects 77

Managing Withdrawal Symptoms 79

Dealing With Discontinuation Syndrome 81

Strategies for Managing Symptoms Long-term 83

Chapter 7 86

Exploring Post Antidepressant Treatment Strategy 86

Conclusion 88

Prologue: Euphoria

The world is a sad place. It permeates every aspect of our life and is everywhere. It is there in all forms, from the grief of a broken heart to the sadness of a world in upheaval. It is unavoidable. However, we may create coping skills.

This book is about learning how to cope with sadness. It's about understanding the reasons of sorrow, investigating the different varieties of depression, and discovering the best approaches to cure them. It's about learning how to live a life of joy and hope, even in the face of despair.

Know that you are not alone if you are feeling melancholy. There are millions of people around the world who are battling with depression. And, there is aid. You can find it in this book. We hope it gives you the strength and confidence to take the measures you need to find relief.

Remember, there is hope. You can find it.

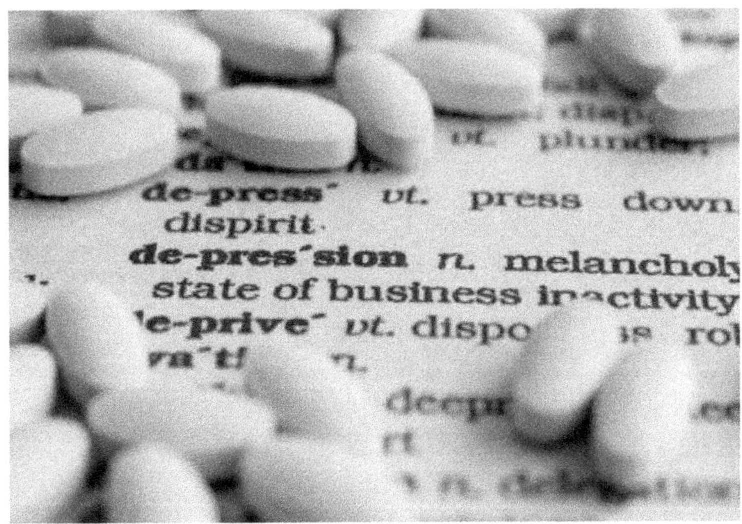

CHAPTER 1

Understanding Depression

Depression is a mental health disorder characterized by a persistent feeling of sadness and loss of interest in activities that once brought pleasure. It is more than just a feeling of being sad or "blue" for a few days. It is a serious condition that can have a negative impact on how you think, feel, and act. It can interfere with your ability to function in everyday life.

The exact cause of depression is not known, but a combination of genetic, biological, environmental, and psychological factors are believed to play a role. Symptoms of depression include persistent feelings of sadness, hopelessness, worthlessness, and guilt. Other symptoms can include changes in sleep patterns, fatigue, difficulty concentrating, and a loss of interest in activities that were once enjoyable.

Depression can be treated with a combination of psychotherapy, medications, and lifestyle changes. Psychotherapy can help people learn to cope with their depression and to identify and change negative thought patterns. Medications can be used to regulate mood and decrease symptoms. Lifestyle changes such as increasing physical activity, eating a balanced diet, and getting enough sleep can also help to manage depression.

If you or someone you know is struggling with depression, it is important to seek help from a mental health professional. With the right treatment, depression can be managed, and individuals can lead happy and productive lives.

Causes of Depression

1. Biological Factors: Neurotransmitter imbalances in the brain can cause changes in a person's mood or behavior, leading to depression. These imbalances can be caused by genetics, underlying medical conditions, or the effects of certain drugs and medications.

2. Psychological Factors: Negative thinking patterns, low self-esteem, and pessimism can all lead to depression, as can unresolved issues from the past, such as childhood trauma, abuse, or loss.

3. Social Factors: Difficult life circumstances, such as financial troubles, the death of a loved one, or a divorce, can trigger depression in certain people. Social isolation, either self-imposed or due to rejection by others, can also lead to depression.

4. Environmental Factors: Certain environmental factors, such as living in a dangerous area, can increase the risk of depression. Lack of access to adequate medical care, good nutrition, and exercise can also contribute to depression.

5. Hormonal Factors: Hormonal changes can affect mood, leading to depression. Hormonal imbalances can be caused by pregnancy, menopause, thyroid disorders, or other medical conditions.

6. Substance Abuse: Regular alcohol or drug use can lead to depression. It can also worsen existing depressive symptoms.

7. Lack of Sleep: Not getting enough sleep can increase the risk of depression. It can also worsen existing depression.

8. Nutritional Deficiencies: Vitamin and mineral deficiencies can lead to depression. A diet lacking in

certain nutrients can contribute to depression, as can eating too much processed food or junk food.

9. Genetics: Genetics can play a role in depression. A family history of depression can increase the risk of developing the condition.

10. Life Changes: Significant life transitions, such as going to college, getting married, or starting a new job, can trigger depression in some people.

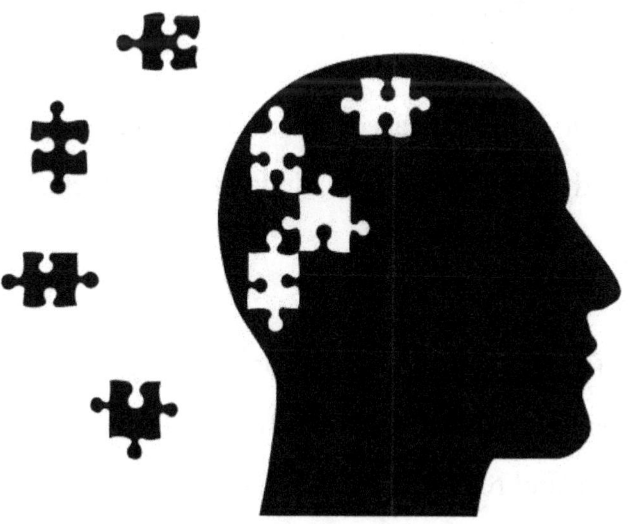

Symptoms of Depression

1. Loss of interest or pleasure in activities: People who are depressed may lose interest in activities that they used to enjoy and may no longer take pleasure in activities that used to bring them joy.

2. Changes in appetite or weight: Significant changes in appetite or weight are common signs of depression. A person may eat significantly more or less than usual, or may lose or gain weight.

3. Fatigue or decreased energy: People who are depressed may feel tired, sluggish, and lacking in energy.

4. Difficulty concentrating or making decisions: Depression can cause difficulty concentrating, making decisions, and remembering things.

5. Insomnia or hypersomnia: Depression can cause people to experience disruptions in their sleep patterns. This can manifest as either insomnia (difficulty sleeping) or hypersomnia (excessive sleepiness).

6. Restlessness or slowed movements: People with depression may feel restless, agitated, or have difficulty sitting still. On the other hand, they may also feel slowed down, with slower movements and speech.

7. Feelings of worthlessness or guilt: People who are depressed may feel guilty, worthless, or inadequate. They may also feel like a burden to others.

8. Thoughts of death or suicide: People with depression may have thoughts of death or suicide, or may make plans to attempt suicide.

9. Irritability: People with depression may feel easily irritated and frustrated.

11. Social withdrawal: People who are depressed may withdraw from social activities, lose interest in spending time with friends and family, or avoid contact with other people.

CHAPTER 2

Overview of Anti-Depressants

Antidepressants are medications used to treat depression and other mental health conditions. They work by balancing certain chemicals in the brain, known as neurotransmitters, which influence mood. Depending on the type of antidepressant prescribed, it may take several weeks for a person to notice the full effects of the medication.

Mechanism of Action of Antidepressants

Antidepressants are medications that work to alleviate the symptoms of depression. They function by boosting the levels of particular neurotransmitters in the brain, such as serotonin and norepinephrine. These neurotransmitters are known as the "feel good" chemicals and are thought to be involved in the regulation of mood. By increasing their levels, antidepressants can help to reduce symptoms of depression. In addition, antidepressants can also help to improve sleep, appetite, energy levels, and concentration.

Classifications Of Anti-Depressants

Classification of antidepressants refers to the categorization of antidepressant medications based on their mechanism of action. This is a helpful tool for clinicians to match a patient's symptoms with the most suitable medication. Commonly used classes of antidepressants include selective serotonin reuptake inhibitors (SSRIs), serotonin-norepinephrine reuptake inhibitors (SNRIs), tricyclic antidepressants (TCAs), monoamine oxidase inhibitors (MAOIs), and atypical antidepressants. Each of these classes work in different ways to alter brain chemistry, and thus are used to treat different types of depression and other mental health disorders.

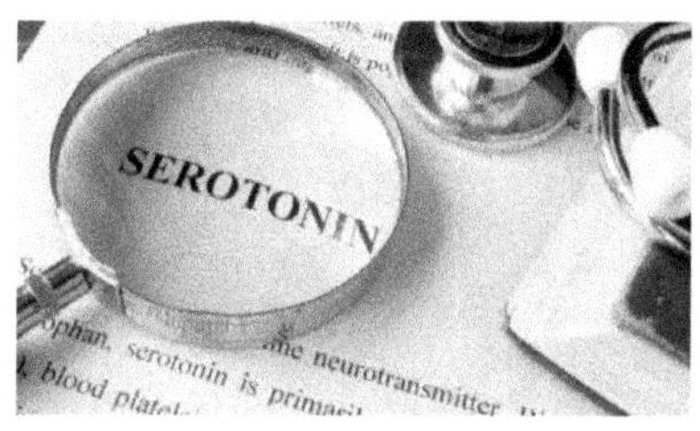

Types Of Anti-Depressants

There a various types of anti-depressants, they include;

1. **Selective serotonin reuptake inhibitors (SSRIs):** These are the most commonly prescribed type of antidepressant. SSRIs work by increasing levels of serotonin, a neurotransmitter associated with mood. Examples include fluoxetine (Prozac), sertraline (Zoloft), paroxetine (Paxil), and citalopram (Celexa).

2. **Serotonin and norepinephrine reuptake inhibitors (SNRIs)**: SNRIs also increase serotonin levels, but they also affect the neurotransmitter norepinephrine. Examples include duloxetine (Cymbalta) and venlafaxine (Effexor).

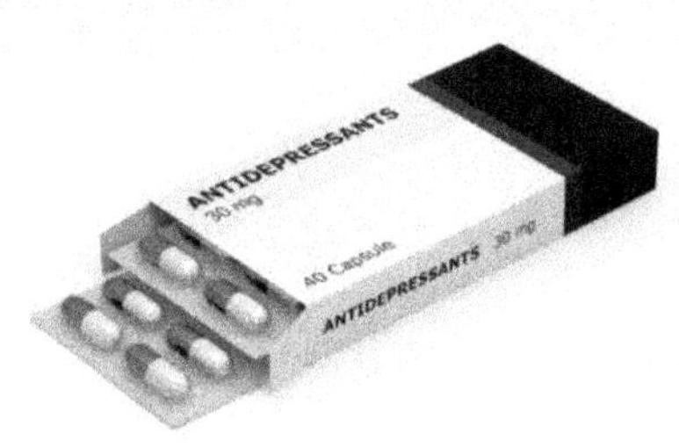

3. **Tricyclic antidepressants (TCAs)**: TCAs work by blocking the reuptake of certain neurotransmitters, including serotonin and norepinephrine. Examples include amitriptyline (Elavil) and nortriptyline (Pamelor).

4. **Monoamine oxidase inhibitors (MAOIs)**: MAOIs are the oldest type of antidepressant and they work by blocking the enzyme monoamine oxidase, which is involved in breaking down neurotransmitters.

Examples include phenelzine (Nardil) and tranylcypromine (Parnate).

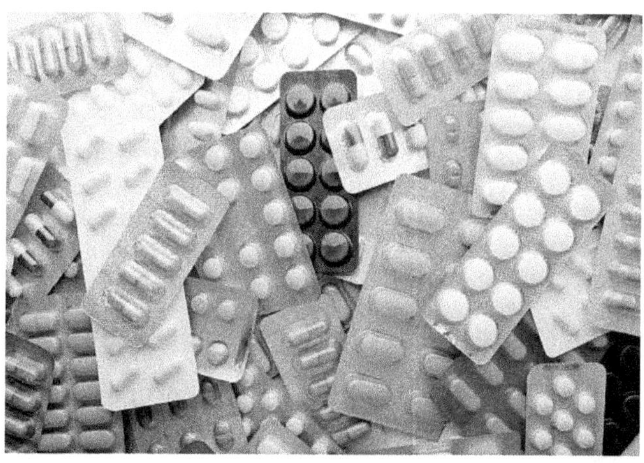

5. **Atypical antidepressants:** Atypical antidepressants are a newer type of antidepressant that don't fit into any of the other categories. Examples include bupropion (Wellbutrin) and mirtazapine (Remeron).

Commonly prescribed Antidepressants

Commonly prescribed antidepressants include selective serotonin reuptake inhibitors (SSRIs), serotonin-norepinephrine reuptake inhibitors (SNRIs), tricyclic antidepressants (TCAs), and monoamine oxidase inhibitors (MAOIs). SSRIs are generally the first line of treatment for depression and are known for having fewer side effects than other antidepressant medications. SNRIs and TCAs work similarly to SSRIs, but they work on different chemicals in the brain. MAOIs are used less often due to their potential for severe side effects, but they can be effective for people who do not respond to other antidepressant medications

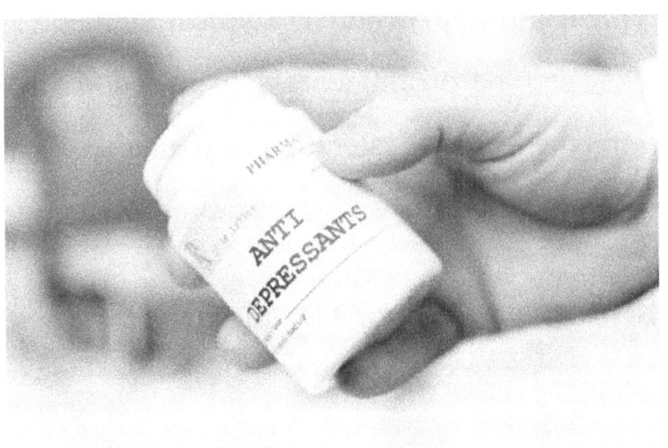

CHAPTER 3

Side Effects of Anti-depressants

Antidepressants are a type of medication used to treat a variety of mental health conditions, including depression, anxiety, obsessive-compulsive disorder, and post-traumatic stress disorder. While these medications can be effective in relieving symptoms, they also have potential side effects.

The most common side effects of antidepressants are nausea, headache, drowsiness, insomnia, dry mouth, and sexual dysfunction. Other side effects can include weight gain, increased risk of suicidal thoughts, and increased risk of serious cardiovascular events, such as stroke or heart attack.

It is important to be aware of these potential side effects so that individuals can make informed decisions about taking antidepressants. In addition, it is important to discuss any side effects with a mental health provider so that they can be managed appropriately.

In some cases, side effects can be reduced by adjusting the dose or switching to a different medication. It is important to discuss these options with a mental health provider, as well as any lifestyle changes that might help reduce side effects.

Common Side Effects

Nausea: This is one of the most common side effects of antidepressants. Nausea can occur when starting the medication or when increasing the dose of an antidepressant. It usually goes away after a few days.

Dizziness: Many people experience feelings of dizziness or lightheadedness when starting antidepressants or when their dose is changed. This usually subsides after a few days.

Insomnia: Insomnia is a common side effect of antidepressants. It can be caused by the medication or by the underlying depression itself.

Headaches: Headaches are a common side effect of antidepressants. They can range from mild to severe and can be caused by the medication or the underlying depression itself.

Weight Gain: Weight gain is a common side effect of antidepressants. It is usually caused by an increase in appetite that is associated with the medication.

Sexual Dysfunction: Sexual dysfunction is a common side effect of antidepressants. It can include decreased libido, difficulty achieving orgasm, or erectile dysfunction.

Dry Mouth: Dry mouth is a common side effect of antidepressants. It can be caused by the medication itself or by other factors such as dehydration or anxiety.

Rare Side Effects

Mania: Mania is a rare side effect of antidepressants. It is characterized by excessive activity, euphoria, and racing thoughts.

Seizures: Seizures are a rare side effect of antidepressants. They are typically caused by an overdose of the medication.

Hyponatremia: Hyponatremia is a rare side effect of antidepressants. It is caused by an imbalance in electrolytes in the body, leading to confusion, disorientation, and muscle twitches.

Serotonin Syndrome: Serotonin syndrome is a rare side effect of antidepressants. It is characterized by confusion, agitation, and high fever and can be life-threatening if not treated.

Long-Term Side Effects

Withdrawal Symptoms: Withdrawal symptoms are a long-term side effect of antidepressants. These can include dizziness, nausea, headaches, and fatigue. It is important to slowly taper off the medication under the supervision of a doctor to minimize withdrawal symptoms.

Suicidal Thoughts: Suicidal thoughts are a long-term side effect of antidepressants. It is important to talk to a doctor if these thoughts become severe or persistent.

Liver Damage: Long-term use of antidepressants can lead to liver damage. It is important to monitor liver function tests if taking an antidepressant for an extended period of time.

Weight Gain: Long-term use of antidepressants can lead to weight gain. It is important to maintain a healthy diet and exercise regimen to minimize this side effect.

Increased Risk of Dementia: Long-term use of antidepressants has been linked to an increased risk of dementia. It is important to discuss the risks and benefits of long-term antidepressant use with a doctor.

Benefits of Antidepressants

1. Relief of Symptoms: Anti-depressants can help to reduce or alleviate the symptoms of depression, such as low mood, lack of energy, difficulty concentrating, and loss of interest in activities.

2. Improved Mood: Anti-depressants can help to improve mood, making it easier to cope with daily life and reducing feelings of sadness and hopelessness.

3. Improved Sleep: Anti-depressants can help to improve sleep quality, allowing for more restful sleep and reducing fatigue.

4. **Decreased Anxiety:** Anti-depressants can help to reduce anxiety, making it easier to manage stress and worry.

5. **Improved Self-Esteem:** Anti-depressants can help to improve self-esteem, allowing for more positive self-image and increased self-confidence.

6. **Improved Relationships:** Anti-depressants can help to improve relationships, allowing for better communication and improved understanding and empathy.

7. **Reduced Risk of Relapse:** Anti-depressants can reduce the risk of relapse, making it easier to manage symptoms long-term.

8. **Improved Cognitive Functions:** Anti-depressants can improve cognitive functions, making it easier to think clearly and concentrate better.

9. **Improves energy level:** Anti-depressants can help to improve energy levels, making it easier to engage in activities and stay active.

10. **Improved Appetite**: Anti-depressants can help to improve appetite, allowing for better nutrition and overall health.

11. **Improved Concentration:** Anti-depressants can help to improve concentration, making it easier to focus and stay on task.

12. **Enhanced Interest in Activities:** Anti-depressants can help to increase interest in activities, allowing for more engagement and enjoyment.

13. **Reduced Suicidal Thoughts:** Anti-depressants can help to reduce suicidal thoughts, making it easier to manage depression long-term.

14. **Reduced Risk of Developing Bipolar Disorder:** Anti-depressants can reduce the risk of developing bipolar disorder, making it easier to manage depression and other mental health issues.

15. **Enhanced Physical Health:** Anti-depressants can help to improve physical health, reducing the risk of physical illnesses and allowing for improved overall health.

Chapter 4

Alternatives to Antidepressant Medications

Fortunately, there are treatments available that have been proven to be effective in managing the symptoms of depression. Antidepressant medications are widely prescribed to treat depression, but there are alternatives to antidepressant medications that may be just as effective. In this article, we will explore some of the options available to individuals looking for treatments that go beyond traditional pharmaceuticals. We will discuss the potential risks and benefits of each of these alternatives, as well as provide information on how to find the right option for you.

Herbal Remedies

Herbal medications have been used as an alternative to anti-depressants for centuries. Herbal medicines are derived from plants, and many of them have active compounds that have been used to treat depression and other mental health issues. Herbal medications have been found to be as effective as some anti-depressant drugs, and they have fewer side effects.

Herbal medications are often thought of as a safer and less expensive alternative to anti-depressants. Herbal medicines can be taken orally, in teas, tinctures, and capsules, or applied to the skin. Herbal medications are not regulated by the FDA, so it is important to research the product and speak with a healthcare provider before taking any herbal medication.

Examples of herbal medications for depression include St. John's Wort, Kava Kava, and Valerian root. St. John's Wort, for example, has been found to be effective in treating mild to moderate depression. It works by increasing serotonin and other neurotransmitters in the brain. Kava Kava is another herbal medication that has been used to treat anxiety, depression, and insomnia. Valerian root is a sedative herb that has been used to treat depression and anxiety.

Other herbal medications for depression include Ginseng, Lavender, and Chamomile. Ginseng is a root that has been used for centuries to treat depression. It works by increasing energy levels and improving mood. Lavender is a fragrant herb that has been used to reduce stress and anxiety. Chamomile is another herb that has been used to treat depression. It has calming and soothing effects that can help reduce feelings of depression.

Herbal medications can be an effective alternative to anti-depressants, but it is important to research the product and speak with a healthcare provider before taking any herbal medication. Herbal medications can interact with other medications and supplements, so it is important to discuss any potential risks with a healthcare provider before taking any herbal medication.

1. **St. John's Wort**: This herb has been used as a natural antidepressant for centuries. It is believed to work by increasing the levels of serotonin, a brain chemical involved in mood regulation. It can be taken in a variety of forms, including capsules, tablets, and standardized extracts.

2. **Kava Kava**: This herb is native to the Pacific Islands and is used as an anti-anxiety remedy. It has been found to be effective in reducing symptoms of

anxiety and depression in many studies. Kava kava can be taken in capsule, tincture, or tea form.

3. **Ginkgo Biloba**: This herb has been used for centuries to treat a variety of health conditions, including depression. It is believed to work by improving circulation, which may help to improve brain function. It can be taken in the form of capsules, tablets, or teas.

4. **Valerian Root**: This herb has been used to treat insomnia and anxiety since ancient times. It is believed to work by increasing the availability of a calming brain chemical called GABA. Valerian root can be taken in the form of capsules, tablets, or teas.

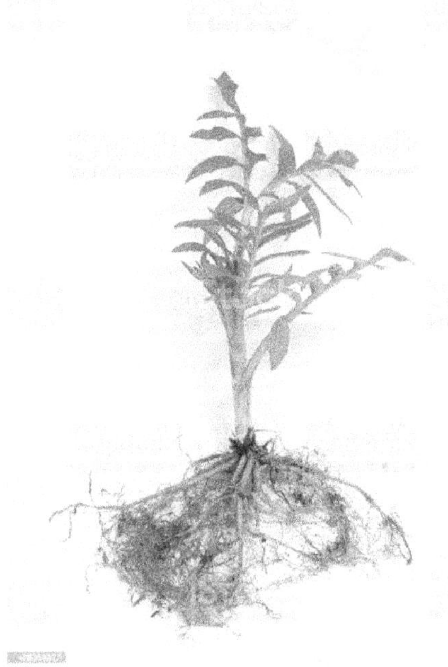

4. **Omega-3 Fatty Acids**: Omega-3 fatty acids are found naturally in certain types of fish and other

foods. Studies have found that increasing omega-3 fatty acid intake can help to reduce symptoms of depression. It can be taken in the form of fish oil capsules or liquid supplements.

Cognitive Behavioral Therapy

Cognitive Behavioral Therapy (CBT) is an effective alternative to antidepressants for treating depression. CBT is an evidence-based approach that focuses on the relationship between thoughts, feelings, and behaviors. It can help individuals to identify and modify distorted thinking patterns and behaviors that contribute to depression. CBT techniques include cognitive restructuring, problem-solving, relaxation, and other methods to help individuals recognize and manage negative thinking and behavior patterns.

CBT has been found to be effective in reducing symptoms of depression and improving quality of life. A recent review of studies found that CBT was as effective as antidepressant medications in treating depression, with the added benefit that patients using CBT did not experience the side effects commonly associated with medications. Additionally, CBT may be more cost effective than medication, as it does not require ongoing prescription costs or other medical expenses.

CBT is not a quick fix and requires commitment from the patient as well as an experienced therapist. It is important to find a therapist who specializes in CBT and has experience working with depression. It is also important to note that CBT may not work for everyone and some individuals may need to consider other alternatives, such as medication, to treat their depression.

In conclusion, Cognitive Behavioral Therapy is an effective alternative to antidepressants for treating depression. It is important to find an experienced therapist to guide you through the process and to be aware that it may not work for everyone.

Exercise

Regular exercise can be an effective alternative to antidepressants. It releases endorphins, which can improve mood and reduce stress. Additionally, it can increase your energy levels, improve sleep, and reduce feelings of fatigue.

For those looking to incorporate exercise into their daily routines, it's important to set realistic goals. Start by finding activities that you enjoy, such as walking, jogging, biking, or swimming. Then, gradually increase the amount of time you spend exercising. Aim for at least 30 minutes of activity per day, three to five days a week.

To make it easier to stick to your exercise routine, create a daily exercise planner. Start by writing down the days of the week at the top of the page. Then, for each day, list the type of exercise you plan to do and the duration of your workout. A custom daily exercise planner has been provided for you below. Additionally, set a goal for how many workouts you want to complete each week.

Finally, remember to be patient with yourself. You may not see results right away, but eventually, you will start to see the benefits of regular exercise.

Daily Exercise Planner

Monday: Walking, 30 minutes

Tuesday: Swimming, 45 minutes

Wednesday: Jogging, 20 minutes

Thursday: Biking, 40 minutes

Friday: Walking, 30 minutes

Saturday: Yoga, 60 minutes

Sunday: Rest day

Diet and Nutrition

1. Start your day with a healthy breakfast: Eating a nutritious breakfast is an important part of any healthy diet and can help set you up for the day. Include complex carbohydrates, lean proteins, healthy fats and some fruit to give you a good balance of nutrients.

2. Eat regularly throughout the day: Eating healthy, balanced meals every three to four hours can help

regulate your mood and energy levels. Try to incorporate a variety of nutritious foods such as whole grains, lean proteins, healthy fats, fruits, vegetables and dairy products.

3. Get enough fiber: Fiber helps slow down the absorption of sugar, which can help to regulate your mood and energy levels. Aim to get at least 25-35g of fiber in your diet each day from foods like whole grains, fruits, vegetables and legumes.

4. Avoid processed foods: Processed foods are often high in sugar, unhealthy fats and calories and can interfere with your mood and energy levels. Instead, focus on eating whole, natural foods that are rich in vitamins and minerals.

5. Incorporate healthy fats: Eating enough healthy fats is important for brain health and can help to regulate your mood. Good sources of healthy fats are fatty fish, nuts, seeds and avocados.

6. Stay hydrated: Drinking enough water is essential for good health and can help to regulate your mood and energy levels. Aim to drink at least 8 glasses of water a day.

7. Reduce your sugar intake: Eating too much sugar can lead to a spike in your blood sugar levels and can interfere with your mood and energy levels. Limit your sugar intake and opt for healthier alternatives such as fruit.

8. Get enough sleep: Getting enough sleep is essential for good mental and physical health. Aim to get at least 7-8 hours of sleep a night.

Daily Diet and Nutrition Planner

Day 1

Breakfast:

-Whole grain cereal with low-fat milk

-Banana

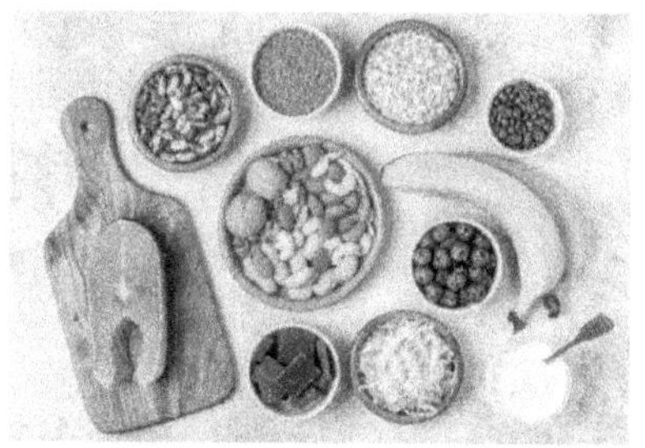

Snack:

-Handful of nuts

-Apple

Lunch:

-Chicken or turkey sandwich with lettuce, tomato, and avocado

-Carrot sticks

Snack:

-Yogurt

-Granola bar

Dinner:

-Grilled salmon

-Roasted vegetables

Snack:

-Dark chocolate

-Fruit smoothie

Day 2:

Breakfast:

-Oatmeal with berries

-Scrambled eggs

Snack:

-Hummus and carrots

-Trail mix

Lunch:

-Vegetarian quesadilla

-Salad

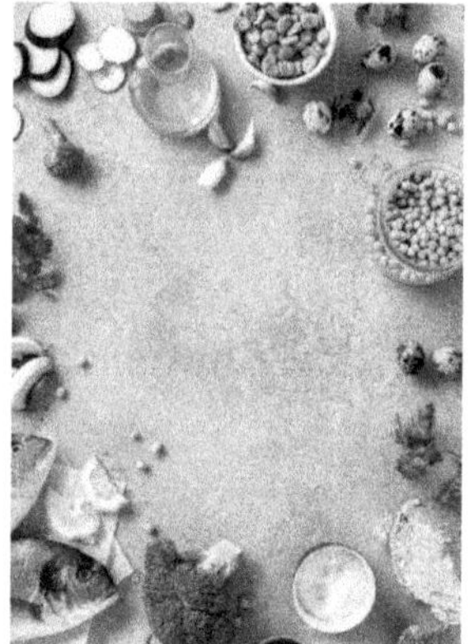

Snack:

-Trail mix

-Apple

Dinner:

-Grilled chicken

-Roasted sweet potatoes

Snack:

-Yogurt

-Berries

Day 3:

Breakfast:

-Whole grain toast with peanut butter

-Banana

Snack:

-Trail mix

-Yogurt

Lunch:

-Tuna salad

-Whole wheat crackers

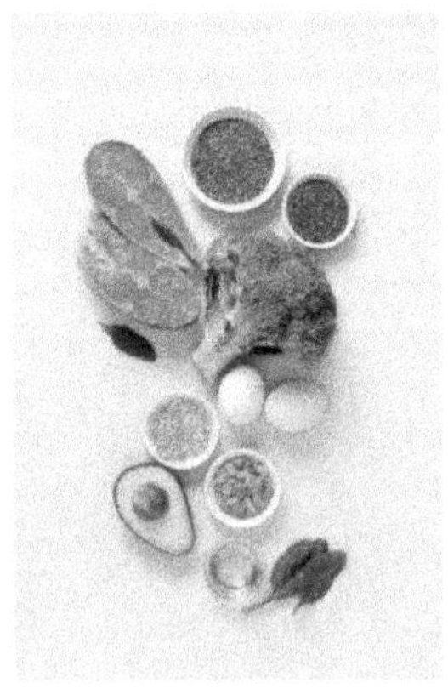

Snack:

-Nuts

-Fruit

Dinner:

-Vegetable stir fry

-Brown rice

Snack:

-Dark chocolate

-Smoothie

Day 4:

Breakfast:

-Egg and cheese wrap

-Fruit salad

Snack:

-Yogurt

-Almonds

Lunch:

-Turkey and vegetable wrap

-Carrot sticks

Snack:

-Fruit

-Granola bar

Dinner:

-Grilled fish

-Roasted vegetables

Snack:

-Yogurt

-Berries

Day 5:

Breakfast:

-Whole grain cereal with low-fat milk

-Banana

Snack:

-Handful of nuts

-Apple

Lunch:

-Veggie burger

-Side salad

Snack:

-Yogurt

-Granola bar

Dinner:

-Grilled chicken

-Roasted potatoes

Snack:

-Dark chocolate

-Fruit smoothie

Day 6:

Breakfast:

-Oatmeal with berries

-Scrambled eggs

Snack:

-Hummus and carrots

-Trail mix

Lunch:

-Turkey sandwich

-Cucumber slices

Snack:

-Trail mix

-Apple

Dinner:

-Vegetable lasagna

-Salad

Snack

-Yogurt

-Berries

Day 7:

Breakfast:

-Whole grain toast with peanut butter

-Banana

Snack:

-Trail mix

-Yogurt

Lunch:

-Veggie wrap

-Carrot sticks

Snack:

-Nuts

-Fruit

Dinner:

-Grilled salmon

-Roasted vegetables

Snack:

-Dark chocolate

-Smoothie

Vitamins

Vitamins can help cure depression, as certain vitamins and minerals play an important role in keeping us happy and healthy. Vitamins and minerals can also help to treat depression by providing the body with the raw materials needed to help regulate mood, energy, and other brain functions. Here are some of the vitamins that can help to cure depression:

1. **Vitamin B12**: This vitamin is essential for producing serotonin, a neurotransmitter that helps to regulate mood. Low levels of serotonin can lead to

depression, so having a proper intake of vitamin B12 can help to reduce depression symptoms.

2. **Vitamin D:** Vitamin D helps with the production of serotonin, and low levels of Vitamin D can lead to an increase in symptoms of depression.

3. **Folate:** Folate is important for the production of neurotransmitters, and low levels can lead to a decrease in mood.

4. **Omega-3 fatty acids:** Omega-3 fatty acids are important for the production of dopamine and serotonin, which can help to regulate mood.

5. **Magnesium:** Magnesium helps with the production of serotonin, and low levels can lead to depression.

6. **Zinc:** Zinc helps with the metabolism of serotonin, and low levels can lead to an increase in depression symptoms.

6. **Iron**: Iron helps to produce neurotransmitters, and low levels can lead to a decrease in mood.

To use these vitamins to help with depression, it is important to speak to a doctor first. They can help to recommend the right dosage and form of vitamin to take to best treat the symptoms of depression. It is also important to make sure that any other medications are not affected by taking vitamins and minerals.

By ensuring that you are getting the proper amounts of these vitamins, you can help to reduce the symptoms of depression and improve your overall mental health.

Chapter 5

How to Choose an Antidepressant

If you are struggling with depression or anxiety, you may be considering taking an antidepressant. While antidepressants can be an effective form of treatment, it can be challenging to know which one is right for you. This guide will provide an overview of the different types of antidepressants and help you to choose which one is best for you.

Factors to Consider When Choosing an Antidepressant

When it comes to choosing an antidepressant, there are a number of factors that need to be taken into consideration. These include:

1. **Safety:** One of the most important factors to consider is the safety of the antidepressant. Many antidepressants can have serious side effects, so it's important to research the potential risks and make sure the medication is safe and appropriate for your individual needs.

2. **Effectiveness:** It's also important to consider the effectiveness of the antidepressant. Different medications can have different levels of effectiveness, so it's important to find out what has worked for other people and what has been proven to be most effective.

3. **Cost:** Antidepressants can be expensive, so it's important to factor in the cost of the medication when making a decision. There are often generic versions of antidepressants available which can help to reduce the cost.

4. **Side Effects:** Some antidepressants can have unpleasant side effects, so it's important to research any potential side effects before taking a medication.

5. **Availability:** Some antidepressants may not be available in all areas, so it's important to make sure the medication you choose is available in your local area.

6. **Tolerance:** It's also important to consider how well you will tolerate the medication. Some medications can cause nausea, headaches, or other unpleasant side effects, so it's important to talk to your doctor about any potential issues before taking a medication.

7. **Interactions:** It's important to make sure the medication you choose won't interact with other medications you may be taking. It's also important to research any potential interactions with alcohol or recreational drugs.

These are just a few of the factors to consider when choosing an antidepressant. Ultimately, the decision should be discussed with your doctor, who can provide advice on which antidepressant is best for you.

Real Life Example

Ruth is a 25 year old lady who has been feeling down and depressed for several months Ohio. After discussing her symptoms with her doctor, they decide that an antidepressant might be beneficial. They discuss the different factors to consider when choosing an antidepressant, such as safety, effectiveness, cost, side effects, availability, tolerance, and potential interactions. After considering all of these factors, Ruth and her doctor decide that an SSRI (Selective Serotonin Reuptake Inhibitor) is the best choice for her. They discuss the potential side effects and interactions, and Ruth is comfortable with the decision. She begins taking the medication and, over time, begins to feel better.

Pros and Cons of Different Antidepressant

While there are various types of antidepressants, each with its own set of pros and cons, they all work by altering the levels of neurotransmitters in the brain. The pros of antidepressants include improved mood, increased energy, and improved sleep. On the other hand, the cons of antidepressants can include side effects such as weight gain, sexual dysfunction, and increased risk of suicide. It is important to understand the potential benefits and risks of different antidepressants in order to make an informed decision about treatment.

Pros of SSRIs (Selective Serotonin Reuptake Inhibitors):

• Usually safe, with little adverse effects

• May be used in modest doses

• It is possible to take it as needed

• It's possible to take this drug along with other drugs.

• Usually well-tolerated

• Can be taken in tablet, liquid, or patch form

• Can take action more quickly than previous antidepressants

Cons of SSRIs:

• May cause nausea, headache, and sleep problems

• May cause sexual side effects, such as reduced libido and difficulty achieving orgasm

• May cause weight gain

• May worsen anxiety symptoms

• May increase the likelihood of contemplating suicide, especially in kids and young people

• May only be partially effective for some individuals

• May help reduce symptoms of both sadness and anxiety

• Usually well-tolerated

• Fewer sexual adverse effects than SSRIs

• Can be taken in pill form

•Can take action more quickly than earlier antidepressants

Disadvantages of SNRIs

• May induce nausea, headache, and sleep problems

• May cause weight gain

•May increase the likelihood of contemplating suicide, especially in kids and young people

• May only be partially effective for some individuals

Pros of Tricyclic Antidepressants:

• Usually beneficial for patients with severe depression May help lessen anxiety symptoms

• Can be taken in pill form

• Can take effect more quickly than other antidepressants

Cons of Tricyclic Antidepressants:

• Can cause severe side effects, such as confusion, blurred vision, and drowsiness

• Can cause weight gain

• Can cause sexual side effects, such as reduced libido and difficulty achieving orgasm

• May increase the likelihood of contemplating suicide, especially in kids and young people

• May only be partially effective for some individuals

Pros of MAOIs (Monoamine Oxidase Inhibitors):

• May help reduce symptoms of both depression and anxiety

• Usually well-tolerated

• Can be taken in pill form

•Can take action more quickly than other antidepressants

Cons of MAOIs:

• May cause severe side effects, such as confusion, blurred vision, and drowsiness

• May cause nausea, headache, and sleep problems

• May cause weight gain

• Has the potential to interact with certain foods and drugs

•May increase the likelihood of contemplating suicide, especially in kids and young people

• May only be partially effective for some individuals

Questions to Ask Your Doctor

This chapter provides a list of questions to ask your doctor about antidepressants. It is important to ask your doctor about the medications they are prescribing and the potential side effects that may occur. This book will provide helpful guidance on what to ask your doctor to ensure you have the best possible experience with your prescribed antidepressant.

1. What type of antidepressant is right for me?

2. What are the potential side effects of the antidepressant?

3. How long will I need to take the antidepressant?

4. What should I do if I have any side effects?

5. Should I avoid certain foods or alcohol while taking the antidepressant?

6. Is it safe to take the antidepressant while pregnant or breastfeeding?

7. Are there any other medications or supplements that I should avoid while taking the antidepressant?

8. What are the benefits of taking the antidepressant?

9. How quickly should I expect to see results from taking the antidepressant?

10. Can I stop taking the antidepressant once I start feeling better?

11. Is there anything else I should know about taking the antidepressant?

12. Are there any lifestyle changes I should make while taking the antidepressant?

13. What are the risks of not taking the antidepressant?

14. How often will I need to visit the doctor while taking the antidepressant?

15. Are there any alternatives to taking the antidepressant?

16. Is there an increased risk of suicide while taking the antidepressant?

17. Are there any long-term effects of taking the antidepressant?

18. Can I take the antidepressant with other medications?

19. How will the antidepressant interact with my other medications or supplements?

20. Are there any tests I should have done while taking the antidepressant?

21. Are there any foods or activities I should avoid while taking the antidepressant?

22. What should I do if I forget to take the antidepressant?

23. Are there any withdrawal symptoms I should be aware of if I stop taking the antidepressant?

24. What should I do if I find the antidepressant is not working for me?

25. Are there any activities or tasks that I should avoid while taking the antidepressant?

26. Are there any support resources I can use while taking the antidepressant?

27. Are there any other mental health treatments I should consider while taking the antidepressant?

28. How long do I need to take the antidepressant before I can stop?

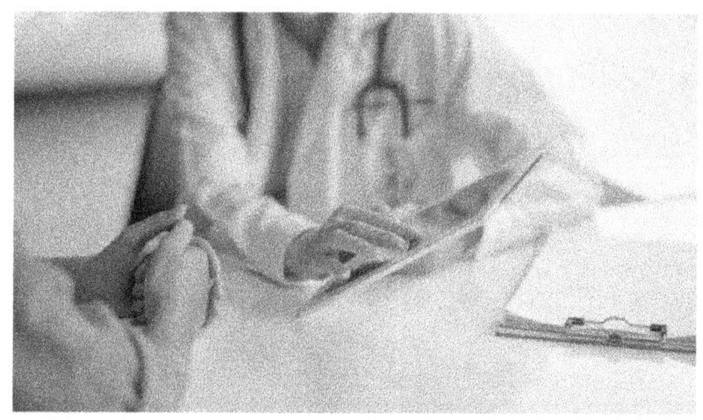

Chapter 6

How To Manage Antidepressant Syndromes

Antidepressant syndromes are a common problem for many people who are taking antidepressant medications. They can range from mild to severe, and can cause a variety of physical and emotional symptoms. Managing antidepressant syndromes can be difficult, but there are some strategies that can be used to help reduce the severity of the symptoms. In this article, we will discuss what antidepressant syndromes are and how they can be managed. We will also provide some tips on how to best manage antidepressant syndromes.

Antidepressant syndromes are a group of symptoms that can arise when taking certain antidepressants. These symptoms include anxiety, agitation, restlessness, insomnia, panic attacks, and an overall feeling of unease. They may also include changes in appetite, weight, energy level, and sex drive. In some cases, antidepressant syndromes may lead to suicidal thoughts or behaviors. Treatment of antidepressant syndromes may include changing the dosage of the antidepressant, switching to a different type of antidepressant, or adding another medication to treat the symptoms.

Identifying and Minimizing Side Effects

Identifying and minimizing the side effects of antidepressants can be a difficult task. The side effects of antidepressants can vary greatly from person to person, and it is important to be aware of the potential side effects when taking any medication. This book will provide an overview of some of the most common side effects of antidepressants, as well as tips on how to minimize them.

The most common side effects of antidepressants include nausea, weight gain, drowsiness, dry mouth, dizziness, insomnia, headaches, sexual problems, and fatigue. Nausea is the most common side effect and can be managed by avoiding rich or fatty foods, drinking plenty of fluids, and taking the medication with food. Weight gain is also a common side effect and can be minimized by eating a balanced diet and exercising regularly. Drowsiness can be managed by avoiding activities that require alertness and taking the medication at night. Dry mouth can be managed by drinking plenty of water and avoiding caffeinated beverages. Dizziness and insomnia can be managed by avoiding activities that require alertness and limiting the use of alcohol. Headaches can be managed by taking ibuprofen or aspirin as needed. Sexual problems can be managed by taking the medication at a different time of day and talking to your doctor about other medications that may be more effective. Finally, fatigue can be managed by getting plenty of rest and avoiding activities that require alertness.

It is important to be aware of the potential side effects of antidepressants and to talk to your doctor about any concerns you may have. Additionally, it is important to monitor your symptoms closely and to adjust your dosage or treatment plan if necessary. Finally, it is important to practice good self-care by eating a balanced diet, exercising regularly, and getting plenty of rest.

Managing Withdrawal Symptoms

1. Monitor and track mood: Keeping a journal of your mood swings and energy levels can help identify patterns and triggers that can be addressed to help manage symptoms.

2. Exercise regularly: Exercise is one of the best ways to manage withdrawal symptoms. It increases endorphins, which can help boost your mood and reduce stress.

3. Get enough sleep: Sleep helps your body and mind heal and cope with withdrawal symptoms. Aim for 7-8 hours of sleep each night.

4. Eat a healthy diet: Eating a balanced diet can help reduce withdrawal symptoms and provide your body with the nutrients it needs for healing.

5. Avoid alcohol and drugs: Alcohol and drugs can worsen withdrawal symptoms. Avoid them to help manage your symptoms.

6. Practice relaxation techniques: Relaxation techniques such as yoga, meditation, and deep breathing can help reduce stress and manage withdrawal symptoms.

7. Talk to your doctor: Talk to your doctor about your symptoms and any other concerns. They can help you find ways to manage them and make sure you're safe.

8. Seek social support: Friends, family, and support groups can provide emotional support and help you cope with withdrawal symptoms.

9. Avoid triggers: Identifying triggers that worsen your symptoms and avoiding them can help manage withdrawal symptoms.

10. If you have been prescribed medicine to help you manage withdrawal symptoms, take it exactly as directed. Don't stop taking it abruptly without talking to your doctor.

Dealing With Discontinuation Syndrome

The discontinuation syndrome associated with antidepressant medications can be uncomfortable and difficult to manage. It is important to be aware of the potential for these symptoms so that they can be recognized and managed quickly and effectively.

The best way to manage discontinuation syndrome is to avoid it in the first place. This can be done by slowly tapering off the medication over a period of weeks or months, depending on the medication and the patient's individual needs. Patients should always talk to their doctor before discontinuing any medication.

If discontinuation symptoms do occur, it is important to be proactive in managing them. Patients should contact their doctor if they experience any of the associated symptoms, as the doctor may be able to adjust the dose or prescribe a different medication. If necessary, the doctor may prescribe a short-term medication to help manage the symptoms.

It is also important to remember that discontinuation symptoms are usually temporary and will resolve with time. Practicing relaxation techniques, such as yoga or meditation, can help to reduce stress and anxiety. Patients should also focus on eating a well-balanced diet, getting plenty of rest, and exercising regularly. Finally, it is important to remember that discontinuation syndrome is not a sign of a failing medication, but rather a sign that the body is adjusting to the change.

Strategies for Managing Symptoms Long-term

1. **Regular Exercise:** Regular physical activity can help reduce symptoms of depression and anxiety.

Endorphins, hormones that can help lower stress and lift mood, are released during exercise..

2. **Healthy Diet:** Eating a balanced diet that includes plenty of fruits, vegetables, and whole grains can help stabilize mood. Avoiding processed foods, sugar, and caffeine can also help improve mood.

3. **Stress Management:** Stress can make antidepressant symptoms worse. Taking time to relax and practice stress-reducing activities such as yoga, meditation, or breathing exercises can be helpful.

4. **Sleep Hygiene:** Adequate amounts of good quality sleep are essential for managing antidepressant symptoms. Establishing a regular sleep routine, avoiding screens and caffeine before bed, and avoiding naps during the day can all help improve sleep quality.

5. Social Support: Connecting with friends and family can help improve mood and provide emotional support.

It can also be helpful to speak with a therapist or join a support group.

6. **Alternative Therapies:** Some people find relief from antidepressant symptoms through alternative therapies such as acupuncture, massage, or herbal remedies. Prior to utilizing any alternative treatments, consult your doctor.

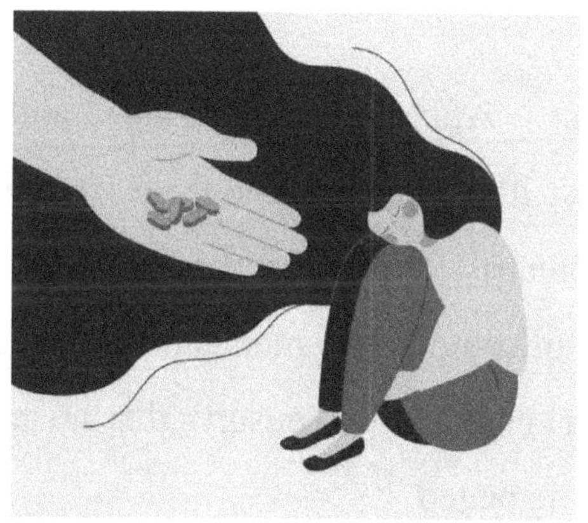

Chapter 7

Exploring Post Antidepressant Treatment Strategy

Post-antidepressant treatment strategies may include a combination of medication, psychotherapy, lifestyle changes, and self-care.

Medication: After discontinuing antidepressant medications, it is important to have follow-up visits with a psychiatrist or primary care provider to monitor symptoms. In some cases, medications may need to be adjusted or changed to ensure that symptoms are adequately managed.

Psychotherapy: Psychotherapy can be used to help people better understand and manage their symptoms and develop strategies to cope with stress and difficult emotions. Cognitive-behavioral therapy (CBT) has been shown to be particularly helpful in managing depression symptoms.

Lifestyle changes: Regular physical activity, healthy eating, getting adequate sleep, and minimizing stress can all help to reduce symptoms of depression. Avoiding alcohol, drugs, and nicotine can also be beneficial.

Self-care: Self-care activities such as journaling, meditating, and engaging in relaxing activities can help to improve mood. Spending time with family and friends and participating in enjoyable activities can also help to reduce symptoms of depression.

Conclusion

In conclusion, managing antidepressant medication can be a challenging task. As we discussed throughout this book, there are many factors to consider when selecting and managing an antidepressant. It is important to consult with a medical professional to ensure that the medication is safe and effective for the individual. Additionally, it is essential to monitor any potential side effects and to seek help if needed. By following a comprehensive plan of care, individuals can benefit from the positive effects of antidepressant medication while managing any potential risks. With education, support, and perseverance, individuals can manage their medication and live a healthier and more balanced life.